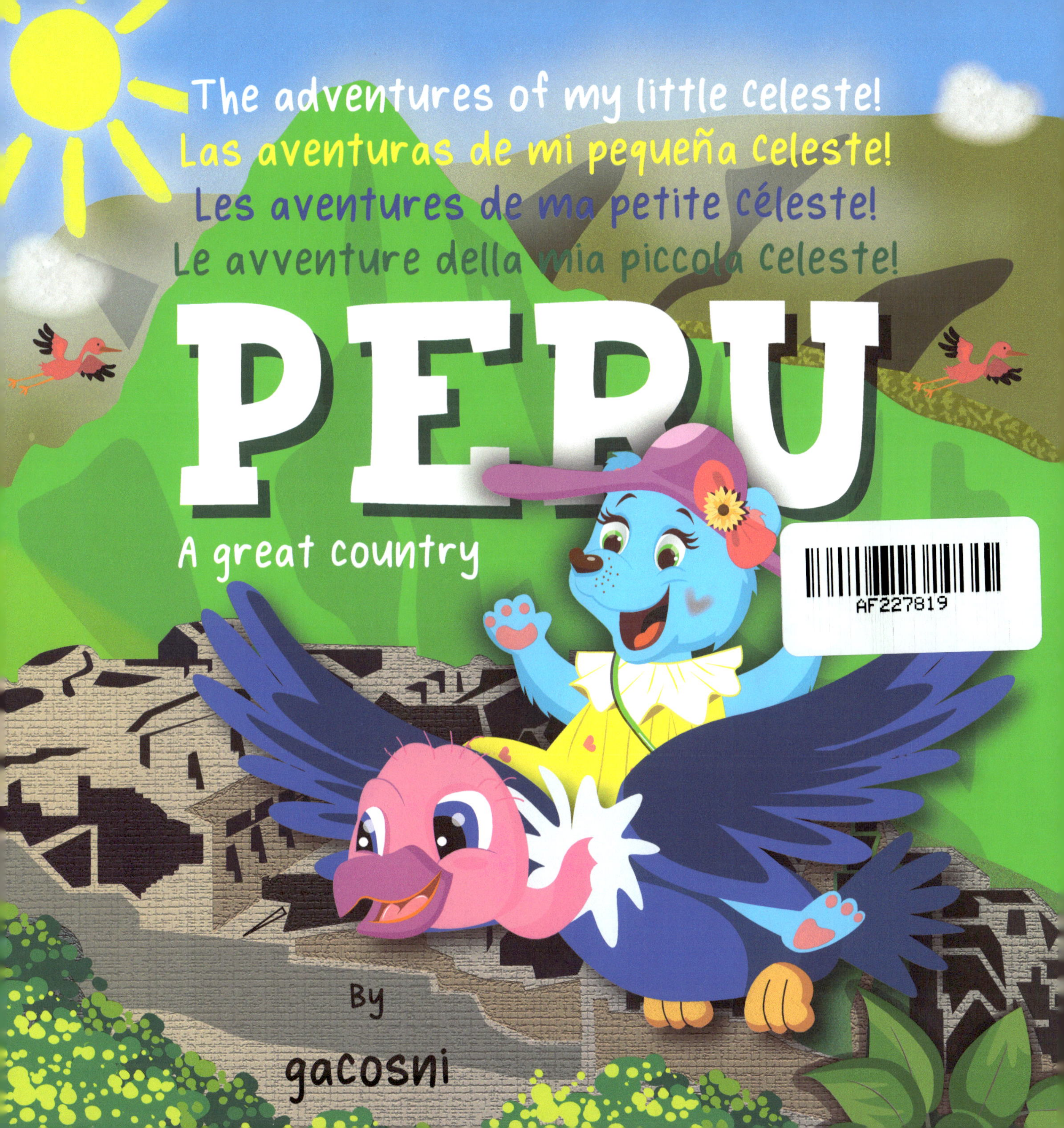
The adventures of my little Celeste!
Las aventuras de mi pequeña Celeste!
Les aventures de ma petite céleste!
Le avventure della mia piccola Celeste!
PERU
A great country
By
gacosni
AF227819

Little Celeste was taking a trip to Peru to visit her Grandma.
Mama Bear helped Celeste with her luggage. Hip hip hip hooray!

La pequeña Celeste decidió hacer un viaje
a Perú para visitar a su abuela.
Mamá Osa ayudó a Celeste con su equipaje.
¡Hip, hip, hip, hurra!

La petite Céleste partit en voyage au
Pérou pour rendre visite à sa grand-mère.
Maman Ourse aida Céleste avec ses bagages.
Hip hip hip hourra !

La piccola Celeste decise di fare un
viaggio in Perù per far visita alla nonna.
Mamma Orsa aiutò Celeste con i bagagli.
Hip hip hip hurray!

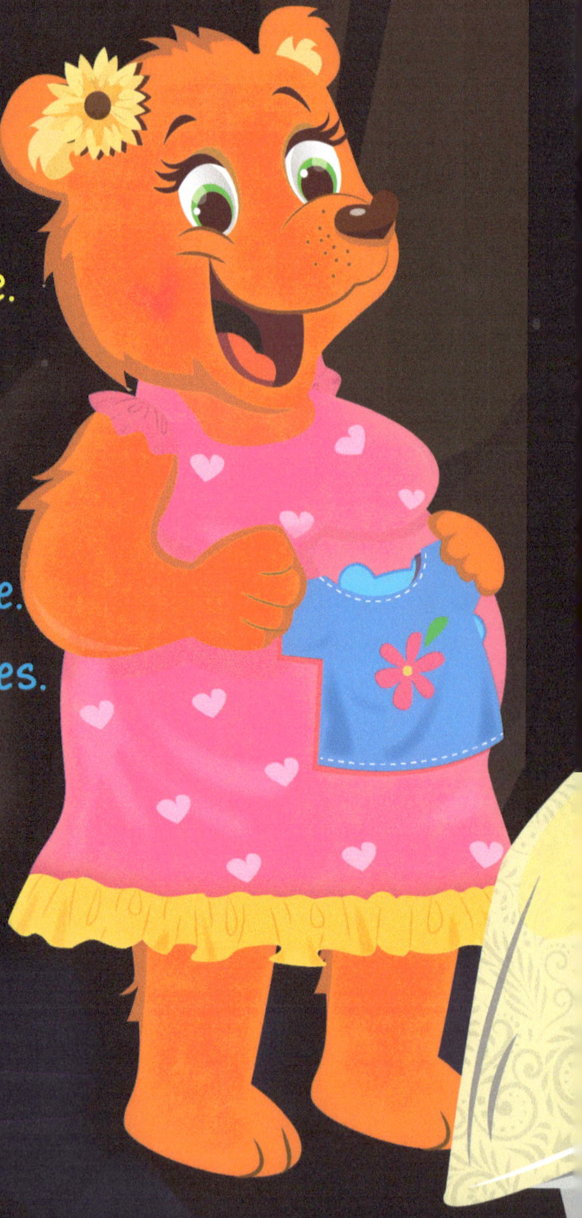

Happy Holidays!
Bon Voyage!
ITALY

Celeste was excited to see her Grandma, but she was nervous about traveling alone. "I could come with you", said Lucy the Condor. That made Celeste happy. It is always better to travel with a friend.

Celeste estaba emocionada por ver a su abuela, pero también estaba preocupada por tener que viajar sola. "Podría ir contigo", le dijo Lucy el cóndor. Eso hizo feliz a Celeste. Siempre es mejor viajar con una amiga.

Céleste avait hâte de voir sa grand-mère, mais elle avait peur de voyager seule. « Je pourrais venir avec toi », lui dit Lucy le Condor. Cela rendit Céleste heureuse. C'est toujours mieux de voyager avec une amie.

Celeste era emozionata di incontrare sua nonna, ma anche preoccupata di dover viaggiare da sola. "Potrei accompagnarti io", le disse Lucy il Condor. Celeste si rallegrò. È sempre meglio viaggiare con un'amica.

As the moon rose, Celeste spied the Northern Lights shining in the sky. Hip hip hip hooray!

Mientras la luna salía, Celeste se quedó mirando la aurora boreal que brillaba en el cielo.
¡Hip, hip, hip, hurra!

Alors que la lune se levait, Céleste aperçut les aurores boréales qui brillaient dans le ciel.
Hip hip hip hourra !

Mentre la luna si alzava, Celeste si mise ad osservare le Luci del nord che brillavano nel cielo.
Hip hip hip hurray!

After traveling all night, Celeste and Lucy decided to stop at Mancora Beach, located in Piura. Celeste remembered the stories Grandma had told her of spending summers at this beach. Now it was Celeste 's turn! As the sun rose, she happily took a cool swim.

Después de viajar toda la noche, Celeste y Lucy decidieron parar en la playa Máncora, ubicada en Piura. Celeste recordó las historias que le contaba la abuela sobre los veranos que pasaba en esta playa. ¡Ahora era el turno de Celeste! Mientras el sol salía, ella se dio un baño refrescante.

Après avoir voyagé toute la nuit, Céleste et Lucy décidèrent de s'arrêter à la plage de Mancora, située à Piura. Céleste se souvenait des histoires que grand-mère lui avait racontées sur les étés passés sur cette plage. Maintenant, c'était le tour de Céleste ! Quand le soleil se leva, elle prit un bain de fraîcheur avec plaisir.

Dopo aver viaggiato tutta la notte, Celeste e Lucy decisero di fermarsi alla Spiaggia Mancora, vicino Piura. Celeste si ricordò che la nonna le aveva raccontato tante storie di quando trascorreva le vacanze su questa spiaggia. Adesso era il turno di Celeste! E mentre il sole iniziava a sorgere, felicemente decise di farsi una nuotata.

Lucy and Celeste traveled all day, until Lucy grew thirsty. "Let's stop here!" Celeste said. "It is the Huacachina, the only oasis in Latin America."

Lucy y Celeste viajaron todo el día hasta que Lucy tuvo sed. "¡Paremos aquí!", dijo Celeste. "Es la Huacachina, el único oasis de América Latina".

Lucy et Céleste voyagèrent toute la journée, jusqu'à ce que Lucy ait soif. « Arrêtons-nous ici !! » dit Céleste. « C'est la Huacachina, la seule oasis d'Amérique latine. »

Lucy e Celeste viaggiarono tutto il giorno, fino a che Lucy iniziò ad avere sete. "Fermiamoci qui!" disse Celeste. "Siamo ad Huacachina, l'unica oasi nell'America Latina".

Amsterdam

Lucy and Celeste set out again, but a moment later, they heard an explosion. It was the great volcano Misti, near Arequipa city. It was erupting! Lucy flew fast to avoid the flames!

Lucy y Celeste se pusieron en marcha de nuevo, pero un momento después, escucharon una explosión. Era el gran volcán Misti, cerca de la ciudad de Arequipa. ¡Estaba en erupción! ¡Lucy voló rápido para evitar las llamas!

Lucy et Céleste se remirent en route, mais un moment plus tard, elles entendirent une explosion. C'était le grand volcan Misti, près de la ville d'Arequipa. Il était en éruption ! Lucy vola rapidement pour éviter les flammes !

Lucy e Celeste si rimisero in cammino, ma qualche minuto dopo sentirono una forte esplosione. Era il grande vulcano Misti, vicino alla città di Arequipa. Stava eruttando! Lucy volò via veloce per evitare il fuoco!

Shaken, Lucy and Celeste decided to take a rest. They stopped at a popular restaurant, to try a famous and delicious dish called ceviche, made of raw fish marinated in lime juice.

With their bellies full, they began their travel again. But a few hours later, they realized they were lost. They had to find Machu Picchu, the capital of the Inca Empire. Celeste knew it was in Cusco, the navel of the world.

Con sus barrigas llenas, reemprendieron su viaje. Pero unas horas después, se dieron cuenta que estaban perdidas. Tenían que encontrar Machu Picchu, la capital del Imperio Inca. Celeste sabía que estaba en Cusco, el ombligo del mundo.

Le ventre plein, elles reprirent leur voyage. Mais quelques heures plus tard, elles réalisèrent qu'elles étaient perdues. Elles devaient trouver le Machu Picchu, la capitale de l'Empire Inca. Céleste savait qu'elle était à Cusco, le nombril du monde.

A stomaco pieno, si rimisero in viaggio. Ma dopo alcune ore si accorsero di essersi perse. Dovevano trovare Machu Picchu, la capitale dell'Impero Inca. Celeste sapeva che si trovava a Cusco, l'ombelico del mondo.

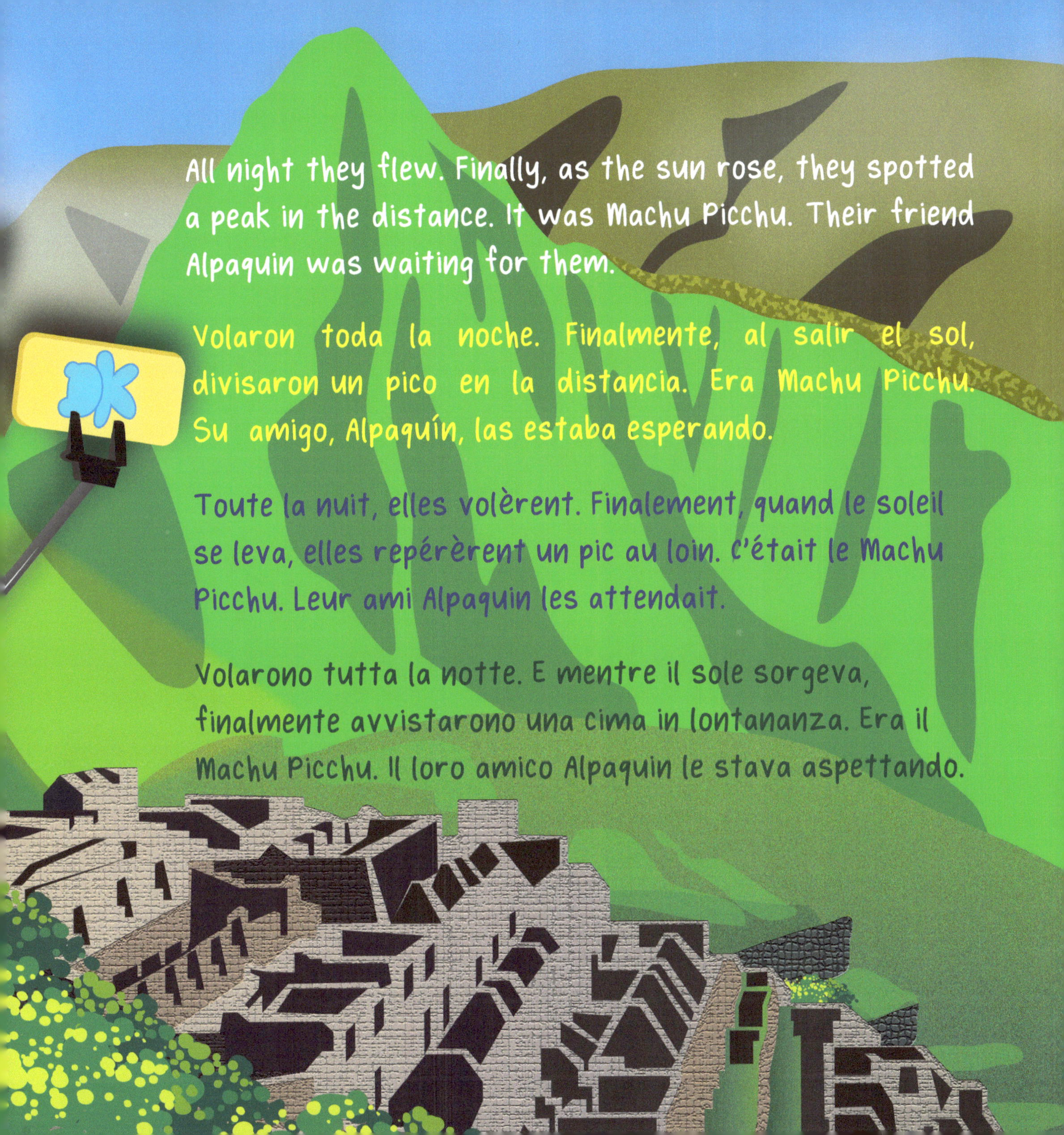

All night they flew. Finally, as the sun rose, they spotted a peak in the distance. It was Machu Picchu. Their friend Alpaquin was waiting for them.

Volaron toda la noche. Finalmente, al salir el sol, divisaron un pico en la distancia. Era Machu Picchu. Su amigo, Alpaquín, las estaba esperando.

Toute la nuit, elles volèrent. Finalement, quand le soleil se leva, elles repérèrent un pic au loin. C'était le Machu Picchu. Leur ami Alpaquin les attendait.

Volarono tutta la notte. E mentre il sole sorgeva, finalmente avvistarono una cima in lontananza. Era il Machu Picchu. Il loro amico Alpaquin le stava aspettando.

El Dorado city, was a short distance from where Grandma lived. Celeste was so excited to reach her home!

La ciudad de El Dorado estaba a poca distancia de donde vivía la abuela. ¡Celeste estaba muy emocionada por llegar a su casa!

La ville d'El Dorado était à une courte distance de l'endroit où vivait Mamie. Céleste avait hâte de rejoindre sa maison !

La città di El Dorado era a breve distanza da dove viveva la nonna. Celeste era così emozionata di arrivare a casa sua!

When Celeste arrived, Grandma Bear and her friends were planning a welcome party. They yelled, "Let's celebrate! Hip hip hip hooray!"

Cuando Celeste llegó, la abuela Osa y sus amigos estaban planeando una fiesta de bienvenida. Gritaron: "¡Vamos a celebrar! ¡Hip, hip, hurra!"

Quand Céleste arriva, Mamie Ourse et ses amis avaient prévu une fête de bienvenue. Elles criaient : « Allons célébrer ! Hip hip hip hourra! »

Quando Celeste arrivò, Nonna Orsa e i suoi amici stavano organizzando una festa di benvenuto. Tutti gridarono, "Festeggiamo! Hip hip hip hurray!"

This is a story about a baby cub named Celeste traveling for the first time to Peru to visit her grandmother. Along with her friend Lucy the condor, Celeste enjoys visiting different places and friends.

During their adventures, they get lost and have a few scary moments, but they eventually find their way to Golden City, where Grandma Bear and her friends are planning a welcome party.

This book is written in English, Spanish, Italian, and French to encourage language learning.

Esta es una historia sobre una cría llamada Celeste que viaja por primera vez a Perú para visitar a su abuela. Junto con su amiga Lucy el cóndor, Celeste disfruta visitando diferentes lugares y amigos.

Durante sus aventuras, se pierden y pasan algunos momentos aterradores, pero finalmente encuentran el camino a la ciudad de El Dorado, donde la abuela Osa y sus amigos están planeando una fiesta de bienvenida.

Este libro está escrito en inglés, español, italiano y francés para fomentar el aprendizaje de idiomas.

C'est l'histoire d'une petite oursonne nommée Céleste qui voyage pour la première fois au Pérou pour rendre visite à sa grand-mère. Avec son amie Lucy le condor, Céleste aime visiter différents endroits et rencontrer des amis.

Au cours de leurs aventures, elles se perdent et vivent quelques moments effrayants, mais finissent par trouver leur chemin jusqu'à Golden City, où Mamie Ourse et ses amis organisent une fête de bienvenue.

Ce livre est écrit en anglais, espagnol, italien et français pour encourager l'apprentissage des langues.

Questa è la storia di una cucciola di nome Celeste che viaggia per la prima volta in Perù per far visita alla nonna. Insieme all'amica Lucy il Condor, Celeste si diverte a visitare vari posti e fare nuove amicizie.

Durante le loro avventure, si perdono e affrontano situazioni spaventose, ma alla fine trovano la strada per la Città Dorata, dove Nonna Orsa e i suoi amici le organizzano una festa di benvenuto.

Questo libro è scritto in inglese, spagnolo, italiano e francese per incoraggiare l'apprendimento delle lingue.

www.ingramcontent.com/pod-product-compliance
Lightning Source LLC
Chambersburg PA
CBHW042143030726

47599CB00002B/593